Sports Stars

TIFFANY CHIN

A Dream on Ice

By Ray Buck

CHILDRENS PRESS®
CHICAGO

Cover photograph: Christie Jenkins
Inside photographs courtesy of the following:
Christie Jenkins, pages 6 and 42
The Tiffany Chin family, 9, 11, 13, 14, 16, 18, 21, 23, 25, 27, 28, 30, 32, 34, 36, 38, and 41

Library of Congress Cataloging in Publication Data

Buck, Ray. 1947-
   Tiffany Chin, a dream on ice.

   (Sport stars)
   Summary: Highlights the life of a Chinese American figure skater, her performances in various competitions including the 1984 Winter Olympics, and her dream of winning an Olympic gold medal.
   1. Chin, Tiffany, 1967-   —Juvenile literature.
   2. Skaters—United States—Biography—Juvenile literature.
   [1. Chin, Tiffany, 1967-   . 2. Ice skaters.
   3. Chinese Americans—Biography.] I. Title. II. Series.
   GV850.G43B83 1986   796.91′092′4 [B] [92] 86-9577
   ISBN 0-516-04361-7

Copyright © 1986 by Regensteiner Publishing Enterprises, Inc.
All rights reserved. Published simultaneously in Canada.
Printed in the United States of America.

R 95 94 93 92 91 90 89 88 87

Sports Stars

TIFFANY CHIN

A Dream on Ice

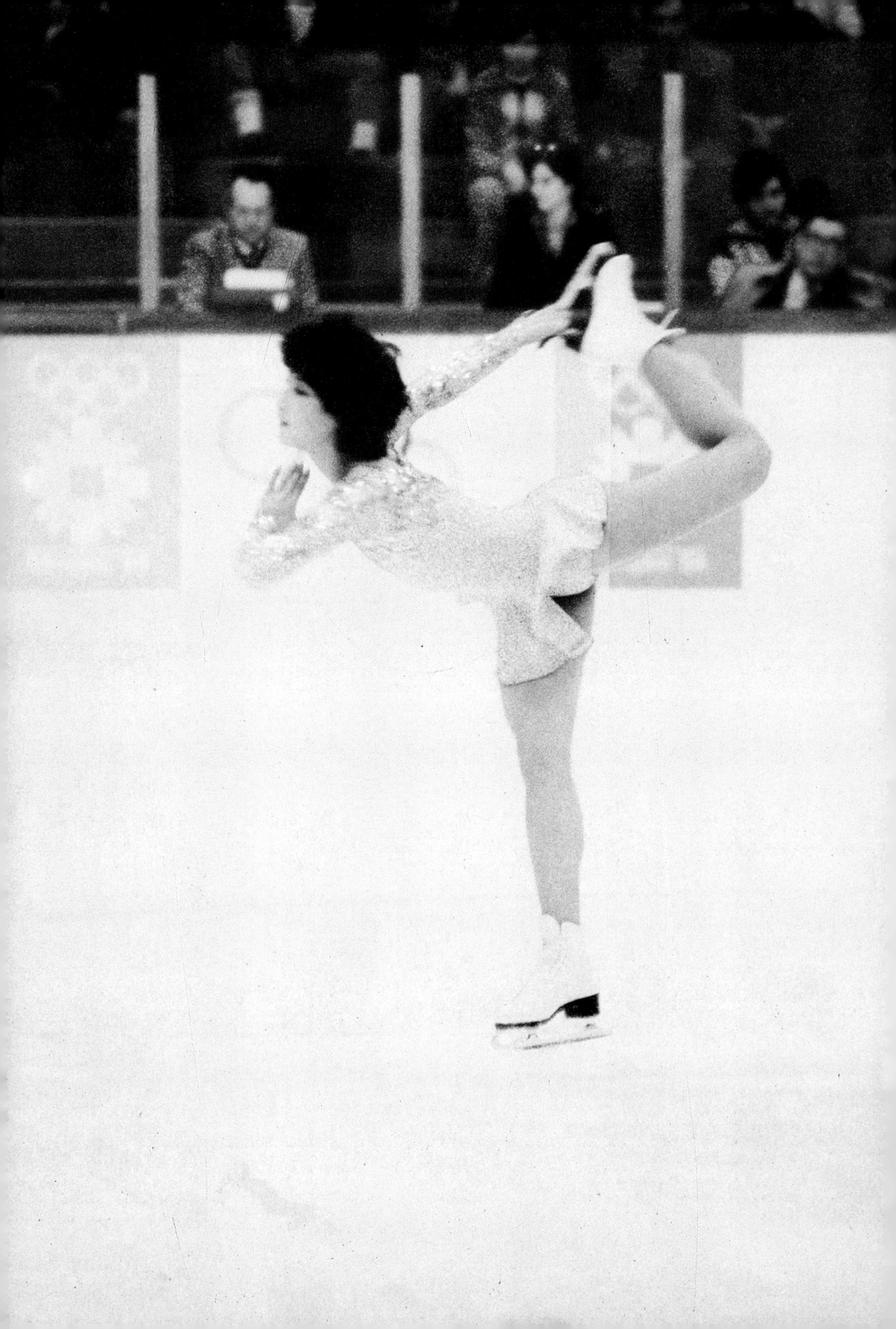

Tiffany Chin began skating when she was eight years old.

Tiffany's mother bought Tiffany her first pair of skates at a garage sale. The skates cost one dollar. Tiffany was proud of her new skates. Oh, they were slightly used, but, they were new to her.

Guess what happened when Tiffany tried to skate for the very first time?

"I remember my first step," Tiffany says. "I fell down."

Tiffany laughs about it now.

"I started out on the ground . . . but I progressed very quickly," she says.

Now Tiffany is older. She is 5 feet 2 inches tall. She weighs 99 pounds. She is one of the best figure skaters in the world.

Tiffany wants to win an Olympic gold medal someday. Do you know what? She could do it.

Tiffany is one of America's brightest hopes for the 1988 Winter Olympics in Calgary, Canada. This will not be Tiffany's first time in the Olympic Games.

The beginning of Tiffany's program at the 1984 Winter Olympics.

When she was 16 years old, Tiffany competed in the 1984 Winter Olympics. They were held in Sarajevo, Yugoslavia. Katarina Witt of East Germany was the best figure skater that time. She won the gold medal. Tiffany finished fourth.

Tiffany lives in California. She has traveled all over the world. She has many friends in many different countries.

"I like the different customs. I like the different languages," she says.

The people in Tiffany's hometown are very proud of Tiffany. She received a special honor after the Olympics. She was given the title of "honorary mayor" of Toluca Lake. That is her hometown.

All Americans were proud of Tiffany's skating in the 1984 Olympics. At a banquet, the County of Los Angeles presented her with a plaque.

They make movies close to Tiffany's house. Many famous people live in her neighborhood. Actor Andy Griffith lives four houses away. But Tiffany does not dream of being a movie star.

"Right now, my only dream is a skating dream," Tiffany says.

So far, it has been a dream come true.

The Winter Olympics—just like the Summer Olympics—are held every four years in a different country. Tiffany must wait until the next Olympics.

But she stays busy. She enters many competitions each year.

In the U.S. National Championships in Salt Lake City in January 1984, Tiffany earned a silver medal.

Tiffany helped in the flag raising ceremony as an honorary hostess for the 1984 Summer Olympics.

Tiffany is looking forward to skating in contests in the future. However, she has been hurt. She must recover before she can skate again. Skating is very exciting. It is also hard work.

"It is definitely a lot of hard work," Tiffany says. "People don't expect a champion to make a mistake."

Tiffany has learned how to handle the pressure. She tells herself: "Tiffany, just try to do the best you can."

That goes for skating. That goes for schoolwork. That goes for everything she does.

Tiffany is not lazy. Do you know how many days a week she practices? She practices EVERY day.

Every day Tiffany practices. Here she works on a trampoline.

She skates before school. She skates after school. She practices 4½ hours each Monday, Tuesday, Wednesday, Thursday, and Friday. She practices two hours on Saturday. She practices one hour on Sunday.

This means she may miss a fun party with her friends or a favorite TV show. But Tiffany knows it takes a lot of practice to become a champion.

"It is like having two lives," Tiffany says. "Maybe not two different lives, but a mixed one."

Tiffany is happy. She loves what she is doing.

Tiffany, her sister Tammy, and her mother

She does not feel she has missed out on anything in growing up. She has always wanted to be a figure skater. To Tiffany, skating is a dream. It is a dream on ice.

"I like skating because of the freedom it gives you," Tiffany explains. "You can jump. You can spin. You can swirl on the ice."

Skating can be fun for the whole family. But Tiffany warns that competitive skating is different. It is not for everyone.

For example, Tammy Chin is Tiffany's younger sister. Tammy likes to skate. But she would rather play the piano.

Michael Chin is Tiffany's young brother. Michael can skate. But he would rather play tennis.

Tiffany and Tammy do many things together. They are best friends. They both received a pair of skates from that garage sale a long time ago. But only Tiffany became a serious skater. Tammy became Tiffany's biggest fan.

"Tammy has never been jealous," Tiffany says with a smile.

Tiffany entered her first competition just six months after she began skating. It was a small contest in Los Angeles. She won! It was her first try. And she won!

Tiffany at age three

Tiffany was very excited. She wanted to try again. Winning gave her confidence.

Tiffany is a small girl with a big heart. She will try anything. She is not afraid. When she was nine years old, she was competing against 12-year-old girls.

Tiffany never has to worry about her weight. She never weighs more than 104 pounds. She never weighs less than 99 pounds. She does not have to diet. She is always in training.

Favorite foods? Tiffany loves vegetables and rice. She does not eat cakes and pies. She will eat ice cream once in a while. But only one scoop.

Tiffany (center) placed first in a competition in 1977. She had been skating only two years.

People call Tiffany a gifted athlete. She is very graceful. She is also very strong.

Competitive skating is difficult. You must have strong legs. You must have good balance. Tiffany makes it look so easy.

Competitive skaters must take a series of nine tests. It usually takes nine years to finish. Tiffany completed all nine tests in 3½ years.

Figure skaters must learn to draw circles and loops on the ice with their skates. They cannot look down. This is called compulsory figure skating.

A figure is skated three times on each foot. The circles and loops must be traced perfectly.

The vice-president of the Republic of China welcomes Tiffany and her parents in June 1984.

Judges watch every move a skater makes.

A skater must have proper form. A skater cannot put both blades flat on the ice. A skater must be able to skate at an even speed.

"It's a struggle to keep your concentration," Tiffany says. "The demands are both physical and mental."

It takes practice, practice, practice.

Compulsory figure skating is similar to playing the piano. A beginner sits down and practices on the same keyboard that a famous pianist does. They may even play the same sheet music.

But the famous pianist sounds better. Why?

A Chinese Kung-Fu teacher, Mr. Wong, teaches stretching exercises to Tiffany, Michael, and Tammy.

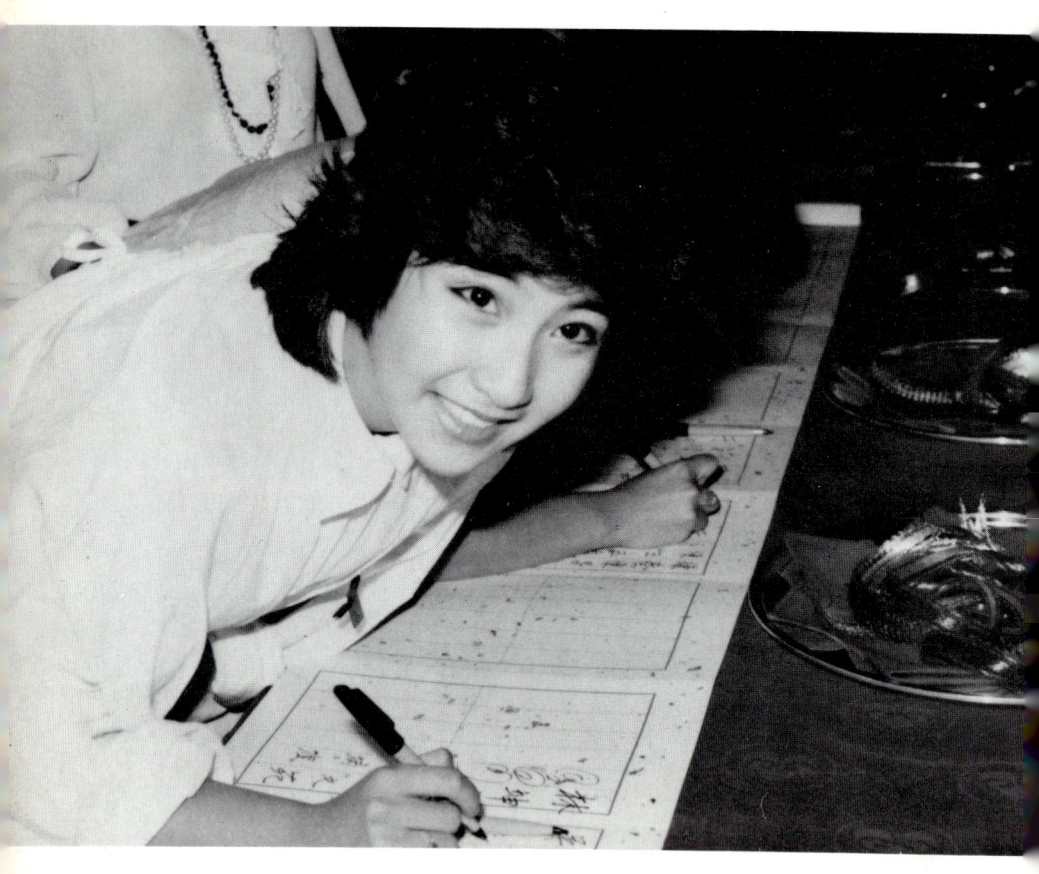

Tiffany signs the guest register at a Chinese banquet.

The beginner is probably nervous. The beginner probably makes a few mistakes. The beginner needs more practice.

It is the same with compulsory skating. That is why the beginner must practice, practice, practice.

There are two parts to figure skating. Compulsory is one part. Freestyle is the other part.

Freestyle is the fun part.

A freestyle skater does a series of jumps, spins, and turns. It is done to music. This is the part you usually see on TV.

Did you know that a good skater can do as many as seven spins in the space of one second?

Tiffany speaks to a group at the Los Angeles First Interstate Bank Athletic Foundation Sports Museum, while fellow skaters, Donna de Varona and Peggy Fleming, look on.

Tiffany is a good skater. She did her best skating in the freestyle competition at the 1984 Olympics. She finished second in freestyle. She finished 12 in compulsory. She finished fourth in the overall scoring.

Tiffany was a celebrity at her school. She went to Providence High School in Burbank, California. She was scheduled to graduate in 1986, but her skating meant she missed many classes. She had to study outside of school to work toward graduation.

But Tiffany keeps too busy to think about being a celebrity.

"My life pretty much has been set on a schedule," she says. "When I'm not skating, I'm doing my homework or I'm exercising."

After a workout, Tiffany takes a break. With her are Hank, a friend and employee of the Ice Capades Chalet, and Leo Freisinger, a former Olympic bronze medalist in speed skating.

Tiffany has a tutor to help her with her schoolwork at home. She has a gymnastics coach and a ballet coach, too.

Tiffany has learned a lot abour her body. She has learned about muscles. She has learned about balance.

Tiffany had problems with her balance on the ice after the 1984 Olympics. She discovered she had a stress fracture of her left ankle.

That happened because Tiffany had overused her body over a long period of time. The same thing happened to her little toe once.

She needed to slow down. She needed to make some changes. Tiffany began to try some new

Tiffany is a celebrity, but she keeps too busy to think much about that.

exercises. They made her muscles smooth and strong. Now she can twist and turn again without hurting herself.

Skating is Tiffany's favorite thing in life. But she is careful not to neglect her schoolwork.

Education is very important in the Chin family. Tiffany's father is a mechanical engineer. Tiffany's mother is a head librarian.

Tiffany likes to read. She likes to read on airplanes to pass the time. She reads all kinds of books.

"Anything with a nice cover," she says with a grin.

Tiffany likes school. Her favorite subject is math.

In 1984, Tiffany had time to dress up and celebrate Halloween with Michael and Tammy.

Skating and school keep Tiffany very busy. But she is never too busy to think about the future—and dream.

She will get married someday. She will be a mother. She will buy her child a pair of skates. But Tiffany will leave the rest of the story up to her child.

"I won't push it," Tiffany says. "I'll tell her about skating. But I will let her do what she wants to do."

Remember what Tiffany says. Competitive skating takes a lot of hard work. It takes practice every day. It takes special talent. It's not for everyone.

One of Tiffany's friends is Dorothy Hamill, an Olympic gold medal skater.

Several past Olympic skaters have told Tiffany, "You are special."

Peggy Fleming and Janet Lynn are two of them. They should know. Peggy won a gold medal in 1968. Janet won a bronze medal in 1972.

Dorothy Hamill told Tiffany's mother, "Your daughter is so beautiful. I can't compare." Dorothy won a gold medal in 1976.

Tiffany has many fans all over the world. She hopes she will not let them down. She always does the best she can.

Tiffany's mother makes most of Tiffany's skating outfits. Does Tiffany have a favorite outfit or color to wear? No, she likes them all. She is not superstitious.

Tiffany is modest. She does not like to show off. She has won many trophies, but keeps them hidden. Most of Tiffany's trophies are kept in the basement. A few very special ones are kept in a safety deposit box.

Tiffany was born to skate. She takes after her father. He is a good athlete.

Tiffany has needed very little coaching.

"Basically, it has been Tiffany's talent," says her mother.

Tiffany's father uses his video camera to take movies of Tiffany skating. Tiffany studies the movies. She is able to correct her own mistakes.

A family photo taken in 1971 shows Tiffany, her mother holding Tammy, and her father.

Although skating is hard work, Tiffany makes it look easy.

Tiffany has a good attitude. She says she always is trying to learn.

"When you think you have the answer to everything, you find you do not have any answers at all," Tiffany says.

In 1986 Tiffany was injured. She was not able to skate for almost nine months. She had to have physical therapy on her leg, knee, and hip. Some people thought she might not be able to skate again.

She did skate in the 1987 United States Championships in February in Tacoma, Washington. But she was upset and did not make the United States team that would make the world tour.

Skating is difficult. Losing can be painful. Being hurt can be painful.

"Everyone gets depressed. All skaters get depressed once in a while," Tiffany says. "You may want to quit. Then you take a second look. Skating is fun."

It is also hard work. When she can, Tiffany must practice *every* day.

"I would rather do that than fall down," she says.

CHRONOLOGY

1967—Tiffany Chin is born October 3 in Oakland, California.

1975—At age eight, Tiffany receives her first pair of skates.

1976—Tiffany enters her first skating competition in Los Angeles. She wins.

1984—Tiffany finishes fourth in women's figure skating at the Winter Olympics in Sarajevo, Yugoslavia. She is second in freestyle.

1986—At the world championships in Geneva, Switzerland, Tiffany wins the bronze medal for the second year in a row.

—In October, Tiffany finishes first in the Skate America competition in Portland, Maine.

1987—In February, Tiffany finishes fourth in the United States Championships in Tacoma, Washington.

ABOUT THE AUTHOR

Ray Buck is a sportswriter for the *Houston Post*. He has covered four World Series, eight Super Bowls, and a few Wild West Rodeos.

He is the author of eight other books. *Dave Parker: The Cobra Swirl, Carlton Fisk: The Catcher Who Changed "Sox," Pete Rose: "Charlie Hustle," Danny White: The Kicking Quarterback, Gary Carter: The Kid, Jim Plunkett: The Comeback Kid,* and *Cal Ripken, Jr.: All-Star Shortstop* are also part of the Sports Stars series. Ray's other book, *He Ain't No Bum,* is about Bum Phillips, cowboy-coach of the New Orleans Saints coach Bum Phillips.

"Tiffany Chin is amazing. She deserves to win a gold medal," says Mr. Buck. "I just wish I could stand up on skates."

921 CHI Buck, Ray

Tiffany Chin, a dream on ice

DATE DUE

BRODART	10/88	10.33
DEC 12 1988		
NOV 13 1989	DEC 06 1990	

JAN 3 1 1989

LONGFELLOW ELEMENTARY SCHOOL